STORK REALITY

Stories from Unplanned Fatherhood

PETER MORRIS

iUniverse LLC
Bloomington

Stork Reality
Stories from Unplanned Fatherhood

iUniverse books may be ordered through booksellers or by contacting:

iUniverse LLC
1663 Liberty Drive
Bloomington, IN 47403
www.iuniverse.com
1-800-Authors (1-800-288-4677)

Because of the dynamic nature of the Internet, any web addresses or links contained in this book may have changed since publication and may no longer be valid. The views expressed in this work are solely those of the author and do not necessarily reflect the views of the publisher, and the publisher hereby disclaims any responsibility for them.

Any people depicted in stock imagery provided by Thinkstock are models, and such images are being used for illustrative purposes only.
Certain stock imagery © Thinkstock.

ISBN: 978-1-4917-0643-5 (sc)
ISBN: 978-1-4917-0644-2 (ebk)

Library of Congress Control Number: 2013916536

Printed in the United States of America

iUniverse rev. date: 09/14/2013

STORK
REALITY

For Jenny and Davis

CONTENTS

BACKGROUND CHECK

I had no intentions of having children. As I write this, I'm looking at a one-year-old boy who they assured me was mine when I left the hospital. I'm still slightly resentful that more time was not spent during the prenatal process explaining that at the end of the nine months you go home with a baby. I had been so swept up in the shock, joy, and consuming anxiety of having a baby that I forgot that the *idea* of a baby is very different from the reality of one.

This new kamikaze family of mine started out in a bar. There were no introductions among friends; there was no prolonged work romance. Instead, a drunk girl walked up to a drunk guy, and fifteen minutes later, we were making out in the back of a cab. A month later, we were laughing and going out to dinner every night in San Francisco. Three months later, there was a pair of socks in my dresser drawer with cats and the phrase "I've got cattitude" printed all over them. Apparently, the girl from the bar had moved in.

Over the next few months, we were in a bit of a fog, what with dining out, drinking copious amounts of alcohol, and feeling generally quite good about having no responsibilities to anyone but ourselves. That's not to say we were completely ignorant in regard to babies and children; in fact, both my girlfriend and I had jobs that put us in contact with children every day. She worked as a nurse in the emergency room of a children's hospital, and I was a social worker who made sure homeless women got pre- and postnatal care—a nurse and a social worker who were both very committed to their jobs but who were also very happy to leave the children and babies at work.

At the time, many of our peers had already begun the planned-pregnancy portions of their lives, and although we happily wished them well, we wanted nothing to do with baby showers and birth announcements. All that changed the night I came home from work to find my living room filled with home pregnancy tests; in the middle of the debris sat a sobbing woman whom I recognized as my girlfriend. In what would be the first of many moments of ignorance, I asked her why she was sitting in the midst of home pregnancy test packaging. My world had just changed, and for the first time in my life I was scared to change with it.

I went in search of some literature to help me feel less isolated in my role of the unintentional father who had no interest in the next big thing in diapers. What I found was a sea of mommy blogs, trendy self-help guides to effective parenting, and that one book Bill Cosby wrote in the seventies. Nothing I found made me feel more connected; instead, I felt more isolated. I wanted to read some stories about people who hadn't planned the births of their children and perhaps had struggled a bit once they were born.

I'm definitely not shooting for Parent of the Year; in fact, I'm hoping that I don't get reported to Child Protective Services. Like most new parents, whether they admit it or not, I'm winging it. The only difference between me and other new parents I've met is that I'm completely honest about my less-than-best parental moments. I have no desire to keep up the perception that I'm teaching my child to play the piano in between sign language lessons. Frankly, I'm just trying to get through the day most of the time.

When my son wouldn't sleep for the first six months of his life, all the books I consulted stated that we must sleep train him by letting him cry for hours. After two days of this, he would supposedly be "trained" and able to fall asleep on his own. This didn't work for me. However, I *did* discover that if I propped up a bottle of formula on a stuffed elephant that was precariously balanced on top of a baby monitor, my son would fall asleep—as long as the bottle remained at a thirty-degree angle in relation to his mouth, the shades were drawn with one inch of light shining in, and I took exactly eleven steps backward to exit the room. My sleep training method has not caught fire yet, but I'm confident that with some quality marketing it could be the next big thing.

Regarding this book and what you are about to read: the chapters are presented in chronological order, but some events might be slightly mixed up due to the fact that my son makes a point of never letting anyone sleep more than four hours at a time. The stories can be read in any order. Each story is merely my sleep-deprived, honest, slightly sarcastic take on what happens when you don't plan to have a baby but are expected to act like the model parent once it is born.

Vodka Baby

A friend of mine, who loved martinis, told me about an old habit he'd had before he'd given up drinking. He would take the toothpicks from his martini olives, and after finishing each drink, he would put the toothpick in his shirt pocket. He did this so he could remember to stop drinking after he had four toothpicks and so he would have some reference point for his total number of drinks after a blackout. There I was, staring at four toothpicks on the table while sitting across from my very pretty girlfriend. I was counting the toothpicks and trying to remember what I was supposed to do after I'd collected four of them when another round of martinis arrived for my girlfriend and me.

In my bed an hour later, I asked my very pretty girlfriend if she was still on the birth control pill. Her response: "No. I stopped taking it." After four—maybe six—martinis, this answer got all twisted around in my head, and I distinctly remember her saying, "Yes, I'm still on the pill. Don't use any kind of protection. Let's just enjoy this amazing moment and ride the roller coaster of new relationship endorphins." I fell into a deep, postcoital sleep secure in the knowledge that my new girlfriend and I would continue to eat out every night and maybe think about planning a trip to Italy soon.

My girlfriend's mood began to have some significant fluctuations about five weeks after the above-mentioned evening of vodka consumption. At the time, I assumed these were run-of-the-mill PMS symptoms rearing their ugly heads for a few days. But after week six, I arrived home from work to find my girlfriend dissolved in tears. "I'm pregnant," she said. My logical, male brain assessed the situation both in the moment and in the context of our entire seven-month relationship, and within .82 seconds I responded, "That's okay. We'll just get an abortion." For some reason, the sobbing intensified. A voice somewhere in my head let me know that I may not have assessed this situation correctly.

We spent the next week talking about all of our options; the possibility of a trip to Italy slowly faded to the background. We decided to make two appointments—one for a prenatal visit and the other at the local abortion clinic. For no reason whatsoever, we decided to go to the abortion clinic first. We walked up to the nondescript building and entered a waiting room filled with teenagers texting on their phones. The boys had baggy jeans and baseball caps on sideways. The girls were dressed like they were hoping to meet their next bad decision in the waiting room.

We quietly found our seats and felt very out of place; it had already been a very absurd day. Our names were called, and we were met by an affable, young social worker. She went through the requisite forms with us, including options for adoption. Then she set us in front of a television to watch what can only be described as a how-to-deal-with-difficult-emotions video. We giggled as we watched the video with its poor production quality, and I think in that moment it began to become clear that we might, in fact, be having a baby. As a couple with good follow-through, we dutifully attended the rest of the appointment, which included a vaginal ultrasound given by the social worker. My girlfriend paused before this procedure and asked the social worker if a nurse or doctor should be the one doing the ultrasound. She told us that she had taken a training class and was able to perform this specific duty. We both shrugged and things commenced.

As we walked back to the car not feeling particularly enthused by our visit to the abortion clinic, I asked my girlfriend why she was comfortable having a nonmedical provider probe around her vagina. She paused and stated, "Well, I've let people with absolutely *no* training into my vagina, so I figured I'd give it a shot." I fell in love with my girlfriend because of her sense of humor, and in that moment of inappropriate humor I knew we were going to have a baby.

It's a strange feeling when you realize you are going to have a child. It's an even stranger feeling when you realize you are going to have an *unplanned* child with someone you've known for a little over six months. You feel connected to each other, but you also feel very *disconnected* from the daunting journey that—until this moment—you had purposefully avoided your whole life. *Would we tell our glorious story of conception at birthday parties and family events?* I wondered.

"And then I had a fifth martini and told her all the naughty things I was going to do to her when we got home. Guess what—she wasn't on the pill! On our first try, we made this little creature that we almost aborted! Who knew vodka was such an effective fertility drug? So tell me about *your* experience. Oh. You planned it after being married for three years and buying your first home? That sounds incredibly boring!"

Fermentation moved to conception, and it seemed my very pretty girlfriend and I were about to find out what was next.

WAITING

When my girlfriend and I made the decision to actually go forward with the pregnancy, I was absolutely terrified after the excitement of the decision wore off. But I did my best to hide my absolute terror. I did this in a number of ways. I played a lot of video games at night to keep my mind off things, and I enjoyed strong cocktails most evenings. I also forced myself to attend prenatal appointments. I figured sink or swim, so why not just jump in and get over my terror?

For my first trip to a prenatal appointment, I was to meet my girlfriend at a very fancy, well-appointed women's health clinic. Everyone I spoke with said that going to these appointments and being part of the process would actually help with the terror.

Unfortunately, no one alerted me to the fact that my girlfriend's appointment had been changed to a later time. When I arrived, I had to sit alone in the waiting room.

There I was—on the couch with a very pretty and very pregnant Asian lady sitting in the chair next to me. We were both reading *Parenting Magazine* because that's what you do, I suppose, when you're an expectant parent. As I was reading "Rainy Day Fun Time Games," I glanced up at my waiting room friend. She smiled at me . . . then ripped a huge fart. Having never been to a prenatal appointment, I had no idea if this was the norm. Do I just ignore it? Do I not acknowledge her very loud and now very stinky fart that had decided to waft over in my direction?

What do you do in this situation? Do you say something like "Nice one!" or "Good job!"? I felt I couldn't just sit there and not acknowledge the elephant in the room, so I looked over, gave her a half smile, and then gave her the thumbs-up sign. Yup. I gave her the awesome-fart pretty Asian lady thumbs-up sign. Like you're supposed to do, right? She gave me a puzzled look, which seemed to be her attempt to normalize the fact that a stranger had just given her a thumbs-up for farting.

Shortly after this amazingly awkward moment, my girlfriend walked into the waiting room crying. I immediately approached her and asked if everything was okay. She responded, "We're having a baby, and I don't even know you."

I wanted to respond with something like, "Oh, don't be silly, honey. We've know each other for years!" But the fact was we'd only known each other about ten months. Some of our fondest bonding memories had recently occurred in Tijuana, when a cab driver tried to overcharge us and my girlfriend used her fluent Spanish to tell the cab driver he was a liar with a small penis. With nothing else to draw on, I brought up this fond recollection and told her if she could stand up to a Mexican taxi driver, then we could certainly have a baby together.

"What the fuck are you talking about?" she said.

"I don't know," I answered. "I'm just trying to make you feel better."

"Why the hell would you bring up that story in the doctor's office? Do you want everyone to know we made bad decisions in Mexico? They're going to think we'll be horrible parents!"

The crying had gone from a few tears to a full-on sob by that point. I'm normally a very supportive person who says appropriate things and is able to comfort those around me. Unfortunately, I was crippled by the fear of being at an actual prenatal appointment. I was in no way ready to accept that at some point these appointments would result in a real baby. I offered a very pathetic hug completely devoid of any real comforting touch, and then my girlfriend asked me not to touch her.

Thankfully, the receptionist wanted to keep some sort of order in the waiting room and ushered us into a holding room while we waited for our doctor to arrive. Sitting there in silence, I think it dawned on both of us how unprepared we were for what we were taking on. Neither of us had taken the time to realize that financial security had absolutely nothing to do with the emotional security necessary to get through this journey intact. The awkward blanket of silence continued to weigh heavily on us, but thankfully there was a quiet knock on the door, and the doctor entered the room.

The doctor, who had apparently not read the chart indicating we were not married, entered the room and greeted us with a great big, "Hello, Mr. and Mrs. Morris!" I quickly let her know that we were just dating. Actually the direct quote was: "Oh, this isn't my wife. She's just my girlfriend." The sobbing resumed and intensified.

At that point, the doctor asked me to leave, and my girlfriend did not object. Given the success of the thumbs up maneuver in the waiting room, this time I gave a double thumbs-up and returned to the waiting room to finish the article in *Parenting Magazine*.

When I get nervous, I tend to speed-read, so in the span of twenty minutes I finished three articles on how to turn ordinary household items into hours of fun. For instance, a shoe box and some clothespins can provide hours of fun for a toddler. My girlfriend emerged from the back of the office. She had stopped crying, and I thought I even saw a faint smile on her face. She looked at me and announced, "I have a yolk sack."

Having no idea what a yolk sack was—but terrified to speak anymore—I just said, "I'm sorry."

"No, you idiot. It's good," she replied.

"Oh, that's great!" I proudly turned to the receptionist who had quarantined us before. In a kind of boasting tone, I said, "We have a yolk sack." She just stared at me, and I could tell she wanted me to leave. We scheduled our next appointment and left the fancy prenatal clinic. Some of the tension was lifting as we walked out to a really sunny day. After a couple of blocks, I thought I would share my newfound knowledge about toddler activities to reassure my girlfriend that I was ready to parent. "Hey, what do you say we get some clothespins and shoe boxes?" She took a deep breath and in a very calm voice asked me to stop talking for the rest of the day. Thumbs-up.

CARRY OUT

I'm from New Jersey. In the summer, as a child, you go to the shore—maybe Belmar, maybe Seaside Heights—but wherever you go, there is always one constant: a huge $2.50 slice of pizza with a perfectly crispy crust and a sweet tomato sauce. The parents on the Jersey Shore give their kids money and tell them to bring back a slice, and they can keep the change for the video arcade. It's a beautiful thing: a symbiotic relationship between the ocean and the pizza, the parent and the child.

With the recent news of my girlfriend's pregnancy still extremely fresh, I started noticing myself observing the parenting tactics of the culture in which I was most likely going to raise my own child. Of course, this was filtered through my own experience of growing up on the East Coast with a practical mother and a dad who liked to throw the ball around. My parents appreciated their children, but they also enjoyed the separation between parent and child. They understood the importance of cutting the cord, if you will.

On the West Coast, I started to notice that parents didn't understand a very simple concept: all you need is a good slice of pizza, and the family fun takes care of itself. I frequent one establishment that provides an excellent opportunity for a laid-back night of entertainment. The pizza is delicious, and they have a garden where they grow some of the ingredients. Unfortunately, this place is a fly trap for every overcompensating parent who wants to show off their skills to other overcompensating parents who just read the latest best seller on effective parenting.

One night, I was trying to enjoy my pizza while my girlfriend and I discussed our anxiety about having our unplanned child. In the middle of the conversation, I noticed a woman with one of those hats that droops off one side of the head (most likely made by a Tibetan orphan), and she started reading aloud to her eleven-year-old. *He looks about eleven*, I thought. *Let him read to himself.* The poor kid is going to come home from college one year for Thanksgiving with the person he is dating, and after dinner his mother is going to say something like, "Are you full? Do you have to make a poopy? A poopy in the potty?"

Shortly after witnessing this mother, the parade of Baby Bjorned dads came marching in. They all seemed pissed off because they thought they were going to be the only ones with the Bjorn on. I swear one guy had a seven-year-old stuffed into his Bjorn, and the kid was like, "Dad, this is weird. My feet are almost touching the ground." When did strapping a baby to your chest become masculine? I suppose right around the same time wearing sandals with socks became all the rage.

There they were—the parents we were supposed to become. Dads were all standing around with babies strapped to their chests while the one woman holding her child looked at her husband disapprovingly for not bringing the baby-strap-on device. You could almost hear her internal, anxious voice: *They are judging me. My friends think that we*

Peter Morris

participate in traditional gender roles. Oh God, what if they think I make dinner and that my husband watches sports whenever he wants to? Quick, say something and let them know this is not true. The woman looked at her husband, then back at her friends, and—in a voice loud enough for all to hear—said, "Honey, I forgot the puréed sweet potatoes you made last night for the baby. Could you run back to our tandem solar bicycle and get it? Thanks, Muffin."

Some friendly advice for these parents from this future dad from New Jersey: get the kids some delivery pizza. Leave them at home. Maybe they will find your porn collection and you can go out and act like an adult. I guarantee you—the children will respect you more in the morning.

.

20

Recessive Features

Here is a really bad idea. On your next scheduled romantic excursion with someone you've known for less than twelve months, discuss your complete genetic history. Forget about the simple stuff you don't want anyone to know about—that you don't have the best aim in the toilet, or that you chronically leave empty milk cartons in the refrigerator. For this exercise, I want you to go deep. I want you to talk about the possible genetic deformity you may bring to your future unborn children based on your relation to a sect of gypsies who resided in western France 290 years ago.

This biological adventure is called genetic counseling, and it's part of any well-rounded prenatal care plan. I was actually looking forward to the process, as I always enjoyed learning about genetics in various science classes. Now, with the impending baby, it seemed like I finally had a real-life application of these arbitrary concepts.

I'm an overachiever in many respects, so I volunteered to go first in charting my genetic history. Parents? Easy. Two healthy parents with no heart conditions and no spinal maladies. Grandparents? Once again, everything was great. Grandpa got prostate cancer and I was informed that I would too, most likely—but that had little to do with whether we should decide to abort our child at this crucial juncture. As we extended out a bit more to cousins and second cousins, it became apparent that my genetic code was intact and there was little risk of some strange deformity hiding in my DNA.

My girlfriend began her genetic review, and I smiled lovingly in her direction. Her parents, whom I've met, are lovely people who were apparently in tip-top shape genetically. Her grandparents both died fairly young and she hadn't known them very well. We shared a moment when I learned she had always longed for a deeper connection with her grandmother. She had died too soon, but it was of natural causes—so we were clear on the midfamily tree. Then she discussed her cousins, all of whom still lived in upstate New York. From what I could ascertain, they all worked in various capacities at the only grocery store for fifty miles. She paused and then said, "My mom once told me that one of my cousins was born with horns."

What the fuck? I didn't mean to, but suddenly I removed my hand from her grasp, and my loving smile turned into a very intense stare. She continued.

"Well, maybe not horns, but two large protrusions on his forehead where horns would be if people had horns. Apparently, he died as a teenager."

I could not stop myself. "Did some angry villagers kill him with a pitchfork?"

The genetic counselor lady audibly snorted at my joke and then looked at my girlfriend, mortified that she had broken some sort of prenatal genetic counselor code of conduct. Then my girlfriend began crying and apologizing to me for having a cousin who had forehead-bump-horn things. I was sorry that she was crying, but I did *not* want to have a son or daughter with horns. I had sat alone during lunch for the entire year in seventh grade because I had been too shy to ask other kids if I could sit with them. I can't even imagine the pain and ridicule my child would endure if he or she approached the popular table looking like a goat.

Thankfully, the genetic counselor had composed herself by that point, and when I asked if we should be worried about having a goat baby, she informed me that unless there were other horned cousins, it was most likely an absolute anomaly. My girlfriend assured me that it was only the one cousin in the family. We kind of limped through the rest of the session, feeling more guarded about our responses.

Later that evening, we had regrouped and were watching a movie at home. I found myself playing with my girlfriend's hair and maybe spending a little too much time running my fingers near the top of her brow. I had always thought of myself as an accepting person until that day. While I would be perfectly comfortable with a gay son or lesbian daughter, I simply would not be able to support a goat baby.

B-Day

I have to be honest: I don't remember large chunks of the day my son was born. I remember being sent home from the hospital two times that day—and the sense of relief I felt each time the doctor said we had to wait for full-on labor. The relief stemmed from the absolute and terrifying reality that I was in no way ready to actually be a father. They don't tell you enough throughout the prenatal process that you're actually going to *have a baby* at the end of all the visits. I think that's kind of sneaky. At no point did anyone grab me by the shoulders, look me in the eye, and clearly state, "You realize that by deciding to have a baby, you will, in fact, be responsible for another human being for the rest of your life." Something like that would have been helpful.

That's what I was thinking about on our third visit to the hospital in a twenty-four-hour period. During this visit, we were escorted to a very well-appointed room. The room had a couch, a hospital bed, and all sorts of fancy medical equipment everywhere. I turned to the nurse and said, "Wow. Thanks for letting us wait in private for the doctor."

The nurse looked at me and said, "Oh, no, sir. It's time. This is your wife's room where—if everything goes right—she will have the baby." A wave of apprehension and fear settled over my girlfriend and me. I had never seen her so scared. I did my best to comfort her, but it was disingenuous at best, as my own selfish fear spread throughout my body. We sat there for what felt like hours in silence, waiting for something—anything—to happen so we could stop thinking about what was going to occur.

Finally, my mother-in-law walked into the room, and she was crying. *How nice*, I thought. *She is so overwhelmed by emotion and the fact that she is about to be a grandmother. She is just letting the tears of joy flow.*

"I just crashed the car into the parking deck," she said before dissolving into tears again. My father-in-law entered the room, his hands covered in dirt and grease.

"Goddamn it! Your mother just wrecked the car again!" he said. "The bumper of the van just fell off in the parking deck of the hospital. I need some rope." At this point, my memory faded to black.

The next thing I remembered was waking up on the fairly comfortable couch and hearing my girlfriend moaning in serious pain. I went to her and she almost broke my arm, grabbing it as she cried out again. The nurse entered with a syringe full of something called Fentanyl. Apparently, this is some sort of party drug or painkiller combination because as soon as the nurse injected it into my girlfriend's arm, her eyes rolled back in her head and she announced she wanted to go to Vegas. I thought this was a great idea, and I'm sure we wouldn't have been the first couple to be in active labor on a casino floor. Sadly, the nurse gave me a look that suggested we wouldn't be playing craps anytime soon.

With my girlfriend finally in less pain and drifting off into a well-deserved nap, I decided to go to the hospital cafeteria in search of some food. I must have looked stressed as I put together a turkey sandwich at the do-it-yourself late-night deli, because a very large and very pregnant African American woman said to me, "Are you okay, baby?"

I turned to look at her and could only wonder why she was wandering around the hospital in her gown when it was obvious she was going to give birth any moment. So I responded, "I'm a little nervous, but shouldn't you be sitting down or something?"

She explained that this was going to be her eighth child and that she knew exactly when she was going to give birth—and it wasn't going to be for another two hours. She told me that walking around the hospital was what helped her pain the most. Then she literally took the bread I was holding out of my hands and finished making my turkey sandwich for me. She handed me the sandwich and said, "Here you go, baby. Don't worry. Everyone is going to be fine." Looking back on this now, I think I must have been visited by a birthing angel, because I returned to the room and felt—well—not as scared.

At some point during the night, it felt like someone had pressed a fast-forward button. Our old nurse was gone, replaced by a new and very chipper nurse. After being awake for twenty-eight hours, I was losing the ability to understand the timeline of the actual birth. I thought the nurse was speaking a different language when she said, "Okay, guys and gals! looks like the doc thinks it's time for a caesarean. Your contractions have gone kaput!"

I personally don't like the word *kaput* in general. When placed in the context of "people are now going to cut open your girlfriend's body and pull your son out"—I *really* don't like it. But it seemed my linguistic preferences weren't taken into consideration as my girlfriend was prepped for surgery.

I was asked to wait outside of the room where the actual surgery would occur. Someone had handed me scrubs and an industrial-sized shower cap for my shaved head. So I sat quietly and kept myself distracted by imagining I was not about to see another human emerge from my girlfriend's body; rather, given my current attire, I looked like I was about to start my new job as a hospital cafeteria worker, so I continued to plan the lunch menu in my head until a nurse popped her head out and said, "Mr. Morris, it's time."

I entered the surgery room, and my almost-new baby's mother was so scared. I sat beside her, pulled out the iPod with the song list we had put together, and put the earphones on her ears. She smiled, and then she threw up on me.

Things got fuzzy in my memory after a nice nurse cleaned the vomit off my sleeve. I remembered hearing the two doctors performing the surgery discussing the NBA Playoffs as they passed what appeared to be a small crowbar back and forth. Then, without any fanfare, they asked me if I would like to see my son emerge from the womb. *Sure? I guess? Not really? Can I meet him later in the nursery?* I stood up to look over the cloth screen that blocked my girlfriend's view of her lower body and found myself looking inside her body—literally inside—just as a long, skinny, purple, bald person was being pulled out, a person who was not happy about what was happening.

I had no expectations for this moment. I didn't know if I'd feel scared, happy, joyous, or some strange blend of all of them and, as I write this, I still can't put my finger on it. I think I was shocked. The room was spinning around me, the baby was crying, and I was being ushered out of the room while the doctors sewed up my girlfriend's—now son's mother's—body. In what can only be described as a handoff, my new, freshly swaddled son was given to me, and I found myself sitting alone in a recovery room with him. I had not spoken any words to him yet; I had simply nodded my head when the birthing team had told me he was healthy and looked great. Now I thought I should say something. I wanted to say something profound, maybe funny, something loving—some first wise words to this beautiful young man. So I started off a long future of meaningful conversations with my son by saying, "What the fuck did I do?"

There are moments when your life changes forever. Sometimes you are very aware of them; other times you can only spot them looking back. Staring at my son, scared to death, I wanted to suspend time a little bit longer, but suddenly there were family members rushing into the room and congratulating the new dad. I glanced around the room hoping to take a cue from the other new dad, but then I realized they were talking to me.

My Gay Dad

Shortly after the birth of my son, I found myself spending whole afternoons calling family members I had not talked with in years to report the joyous news of our genetic code once again being passed on. Some conversations were more poignant than others, such as the one I had with my father's mother about her fourteenth great-grandchild. This conversation was particularly touching, as my father—her son—had died when I was a nine-year-old boy. The new baby represented so much to both of us. It was probably one of the best conversations I've ever had with my grandmother.

My father had died after a three-year struggle with HIV/AIDS, ultimately succumbing to the disease in 1986. This was a time before any kind of effective treatment had been developed for the disease.

When I think back on this time, I remember the sadness of my father's decline, of not being able to see him in the hospital very much, and of the hushed conversations surrounding the reasons for his death. Years later, I would learn that my father was, in fact, gay and had come out of the closet when I was two. He remained friends with my mother but moved to New York City, where, in the early 1980s, it was not a great or rather safe time to be a gay man exploring your newfound sexual freedom.

When my son asks me about his grandfather one day, I'll share the full story with him—perhaps in a teachable moment about why you don't throw around the words *faggot* or *queer*. I'll say something like, "Son, your grandpa loved musical theater, and he would not like to hear that kind of language being used by you." Or something like that. I'm still working out the specific intervention.

In all seriousness, I will without a doubt tell my son the story of my father coaching my T-ball team when I was six years old, right before he began to get more and more ill. You see, my father loved baseball, and he was an amazing teacher, so coaching T-ball and teaching prospective athletes had been a perfect fit for him. Of course, he had his own flair for it. I cannot recall the last time I saw a T-ball game with a man coaching third base who was wearing jean cutoff shorts, aviator sunglasses, and a floral print shirt. If this sounds somewhat peculiar, imagine a table set up next to the bleachers where the parents are sitting. On that table are displayed all sorts of delicious fruit, popcorn, and ball game treats for the kids, provided by my father's friends who had arrived on the NJ Transit train from Manhattan. While everyone enjoys the cornucopia, the friends are making white sangria for all the adults. There is no other way to say it— our T-ball team fan base was fucking fabulous.

My father's absolute favorite thing to shout when someone was rounding second base was—in a direct homage to *The Wizard of Oz*—"There's no place like home! There's no place like home!" Then he would send the runner past third to score the run, while the adults laughed hysterically with my father and cheered their kids on.

As an adult looking back, I remember my father as absolutely gay, sometimes in a stereotypical way. But most of the time, he was just himself and proud to be himself. He was never ridiculed for his Liza Minnelli coaching style by other parents at my T-ball games. My father created a community of parents who had all been there to support their children and have fun in the process.

When my son asks me about his grandfather, I'm going to tell him about baseball. I'm going to tell him how you create a community of people to support one another—and how winning is good, but having a really fine spread of food following a loss cures most of the pangs of losing. If he ever asks, or if the moment presents itself, I will tell him his grandfather was gay and the reason he died. These things, I hope, will help him become a man—that would make his great-grandmother proud.

Unstable Affect

Persistent and consistent sleep deprivation is a bizarre thing. It's not the type of sleep deprivation from consistently drinking too much coffee or burning the midnight oil on a work project. Rather, it's from the day-in-and-day-out grind of taking care of a baby whose one purpose in life, it seems, is to let no one sleep for more than four hours. I know I'm not the first to have experienced this, and I'm not going to tell you how hard it was—because it actually was not that bad. Life just became very simple. Baby cried, we fixed it, we loved him, and then we tried to get some rest when we could. There was one slight problem.

I hate to admit it, but my emotions did in fact play havoc with me as a result of this lack of sleep—more so than from any substance I've ever ingested. Here is a case example: I once spent fifteen minutes reorganizing the refrigerator because I felt that the milk would be easier to grab if I placed it on the left side of the refrigerator. I became so adamant about this that I got into a pretty heated fight over milk organization tactics with my girlfriend. Some highlights of the fight are included here.

"I understand milk better than you!" (I don't understand what I meant by this, but at the time, it made perfect sense.)

"Milk!" (I thought by simply stating the word and then gesturing to a gallon of milk, this would make my point. I had no idea what my point was, of course.)

"I'm just asking for a little support when I try to do something nice for our family." (In my mind, making the milk more accessible was an extremely profound and important thing for our young family's development.)

On the more heartfelt, emotional side of things, I also couldn't predict or control when I might start sobbing. At six in the morning, my son and I would be watching baseball highlights. He had just finished his morning bottle when a commercial came on that featured an incident from the 1992 Olympics. A runner had pulled his hamstring, and his father came out of the stands and onto the track to help his son finish the race. Well, I fucking lost it. I straight up sobbed at the beautiful moment in the Visa commercial, fantasizing about the day my son would fall down at the Olympics, and I would be there to help him around the track.

Thank God for the constant flow of caffeine that became necessary to function and the brief respite a trip to the local café allowed for. One morning, I accidentally put soy milk in my coffee and didn't realize this until I took a sip on the drive home and got so pissed I threw the whole cup out the window. Except the window was not down when I threw it. I constructed the most beautiful and obscene string of expletives. The outburst was directed at soy milk, as if soy milk were a living and breathing entity. It was obscene, downright filthy, and full of spite and venom for all of humanity. Apparently, I had developed anger management issues as well to add to my range of unstable emotions.

There was no use denying it. I began waiting for the paranoid auditory command hallucinations to start—the voices in my head that would tell me the milk is in the wrong part of the refrigerator again and it must be punished. I don't know how you punish milk, but this is a moot point as I was certain the milk would start playing tricks on me.

I feared that perhaps I would start hoarding milk or begin obsessing about how much each person was drinking and measure it at timed intervals throughout the day. I'd keep a journal of milk consumption with perfectly kept measurements cross-referenced with the time of day according to the international atomic clock.

One thing was for certain; my limbic system was fried. I spent my early twenties not sleeping by choice, but nothing compared to this. When I had the opportunity to sleep for eight to twelve hours earlier in my life, I chose to shrug it off in favor of everything New York City had to offer. When my son would wake for the third time in the middle of the night and I would go down to soothe him, it was almost as if he was a little karmic bartender.

He'd look up at me as if to ask, *Were all those late nights and bad decisions worth it?*

The only thing to do was to say, "Hold on, big guy, I'll get you some more milk. It's on the second shelf, three inches behind the butter—pressed against the left side of the refrigerator."

Yukai

I'd been craving sushi since the second month of the unexpected pregnancy. Given the prevailing wisdom in the United States that pregnant women should not eat sushi, I made a decision that during the pregnancy—as a show of solidarity with my girlfriend—I would not eat sushi either. I thought that after the baby was born we would rush right out to the sushi bar. This was not the case, as there was always something getting in the way. Days of craving turned into weeks. Finally, after a seeming eternity, we had our sights set on a local sushi bar we wanted to try.

I was beside myself with anticipation. This not only was a return to one of our favorite foods, but also it was the first time we were going out to dinner as a new family. After spending a good two hours packing the baby bag with every conceivable item—for every conceivable act of nature—we were ready. Nothing was going to ruin my night. We had all the logistics covered. All we needed to do was sit down and order.

Shortly after being seated in a lovely booth, I began to pick up on a possible land mine threatening the evening. A late forty-something jerk of a man was dining with his young Asian girlfriend who sat quietly at his side as he proceeded to be extremely racist and ignorant. I don't quite know how else to explain this person, but I'll give you a small sample of his conversation with the nice waitress from Mongolia.

"You're from Mongolia, huh? You eat a lot of rice then? Oh, you eat meat too? And fish? Wow! We're from Walnut Creek, which is west of here through the *Cal-De-Cott* Tunnel. Let me hear you practice your English and say *Cal-De-Cott*. That's very good! Maybe one day you will go back to your little town in Mongolia and impress the villagers with your English."

Normally, my empathetic self would have flooded with foul emotions, and an interaction like this would have ruined my evening. I would not have been able to enjoy my food in this circumstance, given the level of rudeness I was witnessing. But tonight, my return-to-sushi night, I brushed it off. *He was probably just trying to be helpful and nice*, I thought. Nothing was going to ruin this for me.

Right as my maguro and hamachi were being delivered, my son starting crying—like *really* crying. I'm not a rude person, so I picked him up and went outside to try to soothe him. After about two minutes, one of the waitresses—I believe her name was Sook—came out and asked if she could hold him. I agreed, since the little guy likes to be passed around like a cheap bottle of wine, and I thought it might stop his crying. Then Sook took my baby and walked around the street corner with him. She just left with my baby. So I did what any good father would do in this situation; I went back inside to eat my sashimi.

Upon returning to the table, my girlfriend asked me where the baby was. Actually her words were, "Where the fuck is the baby?!"

Me: "Don't worry! He's with Sook. It's fine."

My girlfriend: "Who the fuck is Sook?!"

Me: "You know—*Sook*, the waitress."

Then my girlfriend ran out of the restaurant in such a hurry that she didn't get to enjoy the very delicate and fresh sashimi with a perfect bowl of white rice. So the racist asshole and I sat there and ate our dinner, while Sook kidnapped my baby. I watched the Mongolian waitress tell the sushi chef in Japanese, "I'm going to piss in his miso"—or something like that. My Japanese is spotty. She may have said, "Can I have another order of rice?" I like to think she did something nasty to his rice to impress the villagers in Mongolia.

My girlfriend came back with the baby, and she was livid with me. She stood by the table holding the baby and glaring at me. Finally, she opened her mouth to speak and asked me, "What the hell were you thinking?" I was so engrossed with my sushi and still so determined to let nothing ruin this for me that I responded with what I was thinking: "I was just thinking I could use some more wasabi."

I knew this was the wrong thing to say. I also knew that an apology would have probably calmed the waters. I rationalized the whole event by congratulating myself for giving up sushi for the entire pregnancy. Of course, my rationalization was not based in reality. The reality was that I gave a four-week-old baby to a waitress I didn't know. Thank goodness children don't start forming memories until age four. At least that's what I'm telling myself.

NIPPLE CONFUSION

Every Tuesday night, my girlfriend gets very excited as she packs the baby's diaper bag for the next day. After seven days of being trapped inside with the baby, she gets to attend her weekly breast-feeding support group. At this group, everyone apparently sits around with their breasts out and talks about all the new baby sounds and developmental milestones that occurred over the last seven days. My girlfriend loves this; she tells me about it every week when she gets back from group. She tells me who cried during group, what baby did what—and I pretend to listen.

"Really? Then the baby rolled over? Amazing."

"You don't say. She is having trouble with her milk production? I hope she pulls through."

Perhaps it's just me—or the fact that I'm a man—but I do not care one bit about what someone else's kid did that week, particularly when the range of accomplishments doesn't exceed a baby rolling over or holding his head up for longer than thirty seconds. My girlfriend has gotten smart lately, though; rather than tell me about the babies' weekly growth, she has started talking about her group members' boobs.

For example, last week I heard all about Frannie's nipples. Apparently, they are very flat, and she has to use a nipple shield to help her nurse. I don't even know what a nipple shield *is*, but it sounds exciting. This week we focused on Erin's ever-changing bra size. Apparently, Erin is having a lot of pain because her daughter is not sucking the milk out of her breasts effectively, leaving them engorged. If Erin doesn't have time to use the breast pump, her breasts go up a complete cup size in only hours. I said I thought that was a neat trick, and she told me I was missing the point of the story. She seemed more pleased with my level of engagement around the breast-feeding support group, though, so I suppose that is a plus.

One Tuesday night, as chance would have it, I needed to provide a ride to breast-feeding support group. At the end of the group, I received a call from my girlfriend indicating she wanted me to come up and meet the new friends she was making. I reluctantly agreed, as I know myself well enough to know that I have a problem staring at women's breasts most of the time. Now I was heading up to a room where the entire focus was, in fact, the breast. It was pretty much a suicide-bombing mission for me.

I entered the room, and everything seemed normal enough. My girlfriend smiled at me and immediately introduced Erin. Her boobs were really small. I didn't understand. This was the woman with the incredibly expanding cup size and, even though I was shaking her hand, I was totally looking at her chest. Before my mouth knew what was happening, the following words fell out of it: "Oh, hello. I pictured you different, Erin." The fact that I had a mental image of someone I had never met was probably weird enough in that moment. This was made even more awkward by the fact that I was staring directly at Erin's breasts as I spoke.

A thought flickered across Erin's face and then her lips turned into a frown as she realized my girlfriend had betrayed the confidentiality of the group. My lack of a poker face—which was still intently directed toward the middle of Erin's chest—was a dead giveaway that my nipple confusion was really a nipple *betrayal*. One of those nipple shields would come in really handy right now to ward off my girlfriend's wrath. There are just some places men should not go, and I can say with the utmost certainty that a breast-feeding support group is one of them.

ATTICUS

As I settle into my new role as parent, I notice I constantly reflect on my early childhood memories in suburban New Jersey. Whatever new adventure we have with the baby, my memory springs to life with long-forgotten pieces of history, and it's really quite nice. One of my favorite memories was the weekly ritual of eating breakfast at the Westfield Diner, where—for the past forty years—breakfast meats have been fried in the grease of other breakfast meats. It was a simple routine. My parents would read the paper, my sister and I would tease each other, a tentative plan for the day was discussed, and then the whole affair was mopped up with pieces of white toast.

Classic breakfast diners don't exist on the West Coast, and I don't know why. Anything remotely resembling a good old-fashioned truck stop diner is corrupted by a blackboard with all the menu offerings handwritten in chalk. Maybe it's just me, but I feel much more comfortable with a sixty-three-year-old former truck-stop hooker with a lingering meth addiction serving my eggs. In the absence of a real diner, my search for a weekly breakfast place to take my new family to had many stops and starts, but I finally found a place that was agreeable. It was definitely not a diner, but they served corned beef hash, so, as in any good relationship, compromises had to be made.

Unfortunately, it was also the weekend breakfast choice of weirdo Berkeley, California, parents who insisted on breast-feeding their four-year-old children at the table. For instance, this past Sunday, I was enjoying my breakfast of corned beef hash and eggs over easy while my girlfriend and I sipped our coffee and shared the Sunday paper. It was totally pleasant and totally delicious, but then I looked up and saw a mother easily in her late forties talking to her son. He said, "Mommy—toast, please," and apparently he wanted some tasty breast milk to wash it down. He lifted up her shirt, and she pulled down her bra. An enormous flash of white flesh fell down to her hipbone, and he just had at it. He literally put his hands on both sides of this gigantic, floppy boob and started breast-feeding. She continued to eat her breakfast and actually looked over in our direction and smiled.

Now, before having a son of our own, my girlfriend and I would have laughed it up over this. But now, when this happens, a very loud and clear voice in my head says the following:

"Oh, Jesus, here we go again. My girlfriend is going to talk about her tits with a stranger."

Sure enough, my girlfriend put down the paper. She made eye contact, moved her gaze to the breast-feeding in progress, and then said something about milk production, pumping, and I don't even know what else—because I was trying to figure out who this person was whom I'd had a baby with. I didn't want to talk to this giant-boobed old lady. She was breast-feeding her four-year-old. This was a person I put into the category of people whom I don't want anything to do with. This was a person my girlfriend—at least the girlfriend I *used* to have—would make private jokes about. She would have used props to mimic the act of taking out a fourteen-inch-long breast that weighed forty-one pounds on its own. But, in this moment, someone I used to know was fully engaged in conversation. She was nodding her head in a shared-experience way, and I was terrified numbers were going to be exchanged.

I soon find out the four-year-old's name was Atticus, and I thought, *What a wretched name.* Thankfully, the conversation concluded without a clear plan to reconnect in the future. On the drive back from breakfast, my girlfriend was giddy as she recounted the conversation she had just had. Then she said, "*Atticus.* What a great name, huh?" Suddenly, I flashed forward to a picture of our family, and there I was in open-toed sandals with thick socks on. The little hair I still had left was pulled back into a long, wispy ponytail. Some sort of world music was playing in the background. In my flash-forward future nightmare, it appeared I'd been corrupted by years of West Coast breakfasts, and my son had friends named Atticus and Rain. I shook the image off and envisioned a fried egg on a hard roll.

POPULARITY

It's amazing how what you think you know about things, or what you say you are going to do about something, completely changes once you start living in the reality of that situation—versus your projection of how that situation should be. Take, for instance, baby gear. During the pregnancy you and your partner make a commitment: no new clothes—we're getting everything used. We're going to build a stroller out of used cardboard boxes and some old roller skates. Then the baby comes. You find yourself sneaking into Baby Gap to buy plaid shorts and a matching sweater. The outfit is going to have breast milk and spit-up all over it in about two hours, but you have convinced yourself your child needs new clothing for safety reasons. Used clothes catch on fire easily, you tell yourself.

Enter the diaper bag. I must admit that I was completely ignorant regarding the diaper bag caste system. Certain bags grant access that, for example, a gray nylon bag from a large discount store does not. This past weekend I took my son out for a walk, and while he cannot participate in playground activities, I still found myself milling about the playground as I got used to this whole change-of-life thing. There I was with my nylon, super spacious, very functional, forty-dollar diaper bag, and I was talking to other caretakers. They also had very large, functional diaper bags and, for whatever reason, they were all middle-aged women of ethnicities different from those of the children they were caring for. I realized that I was in the nanny section of the playground, so I politely said farewell and headed over to a small group of parents standing in what appeared to be the popular section of that particular park.

I can't begin to describe the repressed memories that surfaced upon doing this. It was suddenly seventh-grade lunch hour, and I was making a bold move to sit at the popular table—then I was being asked to leave so that Steve Flynn could sit down. Those mean women on the playground, with their Petunia Pickle Bottom Bags, totally shunned me. Here I was, an affable dad trying to make conversation, and I got boxed out of the parents' circle. I awkwardly walked away with tears welling in my eyes, trying not to let my son see the broken man that was his father.

Yesterday at the mall, my girlfriend and I were walking by the new Kate Spade store. My girlfriend said she would like to have a look at the diaper bags. Fifteen minutes later, my normal, practical, and frugal self happily paid $501.04 for a new Kate Spade diaper bag. I don't know what came over me. Perhaps I was trying to purchase reparative therapy for an experience that had haunted me throughout my life. Or perhaps I wanted to make sure my girlfriend was accepted into the upper crust of playground moms. This would lead to her being asked to chair the day-care bake sale and consequently, my son would go to Harvard, then Stanford, and then he'd go on to win the Nobel Peace Prize.

Most likely, I had simply fallen victim to rampant consumerism, fueled by clever marketing, resulting in some groupthink about the importance of toting clothing soon to be covered in human feces in a $500 sack. Anyway you cut it, though, this coming weekend I'm running onto the playground and organizing a girls' night. We're going to go to the coolest club, order the most expensive champagne, and I'll finally feel what it's like to sit at the popular table. I'm sure I'll wake up the next morning and wonder why I feel so empty, but then I'll look at the new diaper bag . . . and wonder why I felt so empty.

COMMUNICATING

After my time off for the birth of my son, I returned to work and started enjoying the merits of a group commute situation otherwise known as the carpool. Normally, I never submit to activities that put me in small, enclosed spaces with people who have not been properly vetted. But for reasons that defy logic, I found myself in a four-person carpool in which I was primarily the driver. I was also the only male in this group, and—it's important to mention—the other three women were all nurses who worked at a plastic surgery center. Each morning I picked up three nurses dressed in scrubs. We would all say, "Good morning," and begin engaging in surface-level conversation. This was actually highly rewarding for me, as it was one of the few environments in my life that was not completely focused on infants and birth.

Over the past few months, the filter in my brain that usually let very inappropriate things fly out of my mouth had worked remarkably well. Not once in that four months did I mention that our carpool would be an excellent story line for an adult film. Instead, I listened intently to my carpool mates gripe about work—how this doctor or that doctor talked down to them, and how they didn't enjoy being treated like sex objects. Once again, this was a great example of how my filter worked extremely well, as I did not tie together plastic surgery clinic, breast implants, narcissistic male doctors, and female nurses in an attempt to point out how one might expect to be treated poorly in this environment. Nope, I just kept my mouth shut.

Five months passed and our carpool had ascended into higher-level carpool communiqué. On Monday, there was always the requisite check-in about the weekend. One of them usually relayed a good story about a bad date, and I provided them updates on my son's development. Apparently, being a proud father who is able to report on developmental milestones speaks volumes for your character as a man. Tuesday through Friday we discussed television shows and what had been prepared for the previous night's dinner. As the car had become a treasured "safe space," the rapport had grown so strong among all of us that occasionally a subtle sexual comment would be made, and we'd all laugh.

Approximately half a year into our carpool relationship—a relationship that I thought would last for a long while—one of our carpool mates announced that she had fallen in love with one of the doctors and that—while they had been keeping their love affair quiet— he had finally proposed to her, ring and all. I could only assume this was one of the doctors she did not feel objectified by, and if she *did*, then the ring helped assuage the sting of that initial objectification. The car burst into *Oooooooo!* and *Ahhhhhhh!* Having no concept of what planning a lifelong relationship entailed, I simply smiled and offered my congratulations. There was talk of wedding showers, honeymoons, bridal gowns, and many other things foreign to me as my path had seemingly missed that exit on the relationship freeway and taken me straight to parenthood.

On one of our regular Monday drives, I was discussing the merits of the Target baby section—because that was how exciting my weekends were—and I learned that our newly engaged friend was planning to go off the pill and create the miracle that is life much sooner than anticipated. This was explained as a result of her advanced age and a real desire to settle down into a home full of children as soon as possible, as both parties were coming late to their first marriage. I felt I had something to contribute to the conversation, having just gone through the gauntlet of accidental pregnancy followed by our fast-forwarded family development. I listened as she talked about possible fertility treatments that may be necessary, articles she had read on the best diet suggestions while trying to conceive, and a whole slew of other very technical conception issues.

Feeling quite full of myself on this particular Monday morning, I gave her some tips on how to facilitate the process to achieve maximum efficiency in her quest. I went over my suggestions out loud with everyone listening intently. I think everyone was waiting for me to mention statistics about basal body temperature or herbal teas. Instead I went with the following, which was in fact the method that had worked for my girlfriend and me:

So I said aloud, "First, drink four dirty martinis, and finish your partner's third when he or she is in the bathroom. Next, take a cab home and be sure to show the cab driver your boobs in your drunken state. Consider it part of the foreplay. Your partner should fall down while trying to take his pants off and should hit his head fairly hard on the wall. Once you are naked and ready to go, say the following: 'Don't worry, I'm not ovulating. I just got off the pill a month ago, so there is no way I can get pregnant.' Say this at least five times. Have him finish the whole thing with an 'Uh-oh—I think I forgot to pull out,' and then have him pass out on top of you."

In order to truly understand the response to my guaranteed pregnancy method, please insert the most awkward silence you can here. Imagine that silence continuing through stop-and-go traffic, while everyone grows more and more uncomfortable. My filter had failed badly. My assessment of how close we had grown in our carpool was way off, and I had become the perfect example of why you don't carpool with people you don't know very well. As we pulled up to the drop-off location, I was told that nobody would need a ride for the rest of the week—and without it being stated—most likely, ever again.

As a person who does not spend too much time regretting bad decisions, I've moved on from this unfortunate incident. I did, however, reflect on the fact that I may need to start placing myself in social situations that don't revolve around children sometime soon. I think I need to do this for a number of reasons, but primarily it may be helpful to hear people who actually planned to have a baby and family talk about it. Then I can jump right in and tell them about a great idea I had for an adult film.

COMIC RELIEF

Relationship experts say that one of the markers of a good relationship is if a couple has a series of private jokes that they share. Usually these jokes are based on events that occurred that bring up fond memories, and so the jokes serve as a constant reminder of past good times. Unfortunately, I have not been able to find any information about healthy relationships that encourage couples to have a baby after knowing each other for only nine months.

Thankfully, before my girlfriend and I entered into the child-rearing portion of our relationship, we did share a few private jokes. One of our favorites was something we referred to as *kaboom*. Basically, we would wait for a good opportunity to say something really inappropriate, and then the other person would say "*Boom!*" or "*Kaboom!*" upon hearing the comment. The *kaboom* sound represented someone dropping a microphone in a comedy club after a really good joke and then leaving the stage.

Fast-forward to the first time in ten months that my girlfriend and I went out to dinner by ourselves. With no diet restrictions, no liquor constraints, and with baby safely in the care of Grandma, it was time to consume some alcohol and eat food that did not involve a microwave. I should also mention we had been in a somewhat humorless relationship since month two of the pregnancy. We had not made any private jokes nor enjoyed anyone else's jokes in over a year.

Perhaps it was just the result of the overall sensory deprivation we'd suffered while caring for a newborn child, but the food that night—on that first date night in almost a year—was exquisite. *Jamon serrano* wrapped around perfectly ripe white peaches, a baby beet salad with fennel, and brown turkey figs with goat cheese. For our entrees, a filet mignon cooked so rare it was still breathing on the plate, and three exquisite sea scallops that disappeared faster than the martini, two bourbons, glass of champagne, and bottle of red wine that accompanied our meal.

I can't explain how we drank that fast. Physically, I don't actually think it's possible to consume the volume of liquid we put away in that short amount of time. If it were possible for your liver to give you the middle finger, it would have been flipping both of us the double bird.

Here is what happens when you start asking my girlfriend and me what we think about our new baby once we are thoroughly sauced:

Waitress: "So what's it like being a dad?"

Me: "I don't know. He isn't mine."

Boom!

Waitress (to my girlfriend): "So is it nice having your husband at home to help?"

Girlfriend: "What's a husband? You mean people get married before kids?"

Boom!

Waitress (not laughing): "So is this your first child?"

Both of us: "First one we kept!"

Kaboom!

In the cab ride home a strange and mysterious feeling descended upon us. I had a sense of elation, a tingling feeling in my legs, a longing to actually kiss my girlfriend. With the alcohol serving as a truth serum, it all just poured out of us—how much we loved each other but that we got into this way too fast. We shared our sadness on never getting to finish our courting period and not truly being ready for parenthood. We kissed in the back of the cab like kids on a date. *I love you* was mentioned more than once. Underlying all of it was the anticipation that for the first time in months, we were going to have sex . . . with the other person.

Returning home, we entered a house that looked like a sitcom set—or at least it did when viewed through the gallon of booze we had consumed. There were four different types of formula bottles in the sink, a jumpy on the door, another jumpy on the floor, blue blankets, fuzzy blankets, laundry piled on the kitchen table—and the whole house smelled of baby powder. Grandma took us through the play-by-play of the evening: the goos and gaas, a blow-by-blow about bath time, and then a short list of items we would need to pick up the next day. We closed the door behind Grandma and began to clean up the kitchen. I made a bottle for a possible late-night wake-up and feeding.

Me: "I'm pretty tired. I think I'm going to go to bed."

Girlfriend: "Me too. Good night."

(*Boom.*)

MADAME BUTTERFLY

I'm quickly learning that getting your child placed in a quality day-care center is an extremely competitive process. My child can't even sit up yet, but I've already started calling around to get a sense of the various places, personalities, waiting lists, prices, and so forth. I had actually lived a blissfully ignorant existence around child-care issues, until I heard a report on National Public Radio.

NPR had recently aired a series on gender identity and all things transgendered, but the focus was on children. They ran a story about a father on a "journey" to accept that his four-year-old son was actually his four-year-old daughter. The story went on, and I didn't learn a lot about the child, but it was painfully obvious how proud the parent was that he had completely accepted his child. He had become a modern-day parent and embraced the diversity that his child had brought to his family. His child liked to wear dresses, play with dolls, and was now called Victoria instead of Joseph. I have male friends in their thirties who dress up as women occasionally, so I was slightly underwhelmed by this achievement. If my son wants to unleash his inner woman, I will support him until the day he dies—but I won't need to go on the radio and talk about it.

It did occur to me, though, that this was the parent/child combo my kid was going to be competing against to get placement in a premium day-care center. What San Francisco Bay Area preschool doesn't want a little transgendered child on the playground to up their overall diversity rating? Last night I burned the midnight oil trying to come up with a good interview monologue to deliver when we would be asked what our son would bring to the day-care experience. Here is what I've got so far:

"Well, first of all, we don't refer to our child as our son or daughter. Instead we call it *lumpungo*, which is an African word for butterfly. We feel that lumpungo embodies what we are all trying to do, which is evolve—to become something different from what we thought we were. I think it's also important to mention that we think lumpungo may be gay, which would be a blessing. I'm currently working on teaching lumpungo to play the harp while communicating through American Sign Language at the same time. What I'm saying to you is: if you accept lumpungo into your school, you'll be one of the few Bay Area preschools with a gay, harp-playing butterfly."

The alternative is to just go with the truth, but I don't think a preschool with its manufactured fairy-tale atmosphere wants to hear the reality of how some of its clients got there. In all honesty, I would love to walk into the interview with the school admissions counselor—who never stops smiling—and tell her why we need to be accepted into her school.

"So here is the deal, lady. I understand you are upset with my girlfriend and me for giving you an application only five months before we are hoping to get our child into your facility. You keep saying if we were prepared and did our homework a little better, we would have had the application in at least eighteen months before the child was ready to enter. Do you know what we were doing eighteen months ago? We were in Tijuana, Mexico, getting cheap tequila poured down our throats while ugly women with nice breasts blew whistles in our ears. After the tequila, we wandered into a *pharmacia* to get some pain relief for my sudden back injury, which required six Percocets, four Klonopins, and eighty milligrams of Oxycontin. While we walked down a street in Tijuana that reeked of urine, I thought to myself, "You know what, honey? We should get our unborn, not-yet-created child on a waiting list for day care."

Bring it on, transgendered baby. It would probably be illegal for NPR to broadcast the diversity *our* family brings to the table.

GRADUATION

I have accepted that I can be very much the antiparent sometimes; events that normal parents look forward to occasionally make me nauseous, such as searching for and interviewing at preschools when it was time for our little baby to enter full-time child care. Having not applied two years before my son was conceived, we were stuck with the more expensive schools that prey on the unprepared parent. As I began the tour of a particular facility, I looked around at the eager mothers and fathers armed with their prepared questions. That is to say—statements posed as questions, designed to display their knowledge of early childhood development rather than evoke some sort of meaningful answer. "Are the teachers here familiar with Erickson's stages of development?" Before an answer was even given, the other parents silently nodded their approval of such a great question, which made the asker feel all the more like an expert.

I turned the volume down in my brain and noticed a particularly snotty child talking to a small turtle in a tank. Snot Bucket sensed me watching him and immediately made a beeline for me.

"That's Shelly!" He pointed at the turtle. "Shelly is a turtle."

"Thanks for clearing that up," I responded.

"You're welcome!" he said.

I supposed Snot Bucket felt as if we had established a sufficient amount of rapport, and so he decided to just let it all out.

"My dad lives in New York City with a girl. I was just visiting him for two weeks. My mom cries a lot and said my dad is trying to relive his youth. I told my mom we should get him a turtle and a robot."

Who knew that Snot Bucket was so full of information about the nature of interpersonal relationships? As much as it pained me to leave him, I had to keep up with the rest of the tour. As we rounded the corner to the next classroom, we began what I like to call the child-sex-offender portion of the tour. Ten little boys and girls were all lined up in front of five miniature toilets, and they practiced the various skills of going pee-pee in the potty. Apparently, this was not a coincidence but rather a clever marketing ploy to let parents know that for an additional $125 a month, the one-year-old class could start potty training early. This was all being explained while children practiced taking their pants on and off.

Moving on, it was time for the teachers to explain the curriculum and the importance of circle time. Rather than have us observe circle time and watch the children sing and play "Duck, Duck, Goose," we were invited to sit and participate in an experiential group. The ten of us on the tour were made to sit in a circle, and we had to introduce ourselves by saying our names and something we liked. The tricky part was that both your name and the thing you liked had to rhyme. I knew at this point that I had entered a hell especially reserved for people like me—people who had done a ton of drugs in their twenties and then had the audacity to become a parent in their thirties. Dave began.

"My name is Dave, and I like waves."

It seemed Dave liked surfing. All but me responded with, "Hi, Dave!"

Next it was Barbara. "My name is Barb, and I like to farm."

I personally thought *Barb* and *farm* were kind of a stretch, but we had to be supportive in circle time. So it was my turn to play the game. I didn't want to play and be part of a circle that I was growing increasingly uncomfortable in. I sighed and gave it a shot.

"My name is Peter, and I like cheese."

The tour guide/teacher person made a frowny clown face at me and said, "I don't think you understood the assignment, Peter. Would you like to try again?"

I understood the assignment just fine. I think what I didn't understand was how I went from drinking martinis in a bar to looking at preschools with Dave and Barb. I stood up from circle time and walked slowly to the parking lot. This school did not seem like a good fit but neither did having a baby with someone I had known less than a year. My final thought that day was how on earth would I respond to my girlfriend's question that morning: "Honey, do you want to have another baby with me?" I had no logical answer for this earlier in the day or now. Then I smiled a bit as it occurred to me that I had not made a logical decision in well over eighteen months. The baby is healthy, my girlfriend and I are happy, and how much more work could two kids possibly be?